X-TREME FACTS: NATURAL DISASTERS

TORNADOES

by Marcia Abramson

BEARPORT
PUBLISHING

Minneapolis, Minnesota

Credits:
Title Page, Minerva Studio/Shutterstock; 4, vchal/Shutterstock; 4 top, Singh Virender/Shutterstock; 4 bottom left, 4 bottom right, SteffenWalter/Shutterstock.com; 5 top, solarseven/Shutterstock; 5 top middle, MrSegui/Shutterstock.com; 5 bottom, 8, 9 top, 15 top, 15 bottom, Cammie Czuchnicki/Shutterstock; 5 bottom middle, Earth Trotter Photography/Shutterstock; 5 bottom left, Stock-Asso/Shutterstock; 5 bottom right, NicoElNino/Shutterstock; 6, Laura Hedien/Shutterstock; 6 bottom left, 10 left, 10 right, 13 bottom right, 15 top left, 15 bottom middle, LightField Studios/Shutterstock; 6 bottom right, Pedro Lira Rencoret/Public Domain; 7 top, Todd Shoemake/Shutterstock; 7 top left, Public Domain; 7 middle left, swa182/Shutterstock; 7 middle right, Huntstyle/Shutterstock; 7 bottom, 12 middle left, 12 bottom, National Weather Service/Public Domain; 7 bottom right, Geofox/Shutterstock.com; 8 bottom left, Juice Flair/Shutterstock; 9 bottom, Pikoso.kz/Shutterstock; 9 bottom left, Allison C Bailey/Shutterstock.com; 9 bottom right, 15 top right, 23 bottom left, 27 top left, Roman Samborskyi/Shutterstock; p 10, Jennifer Princ/Shutterstock; 11 top, 11 bottom, 13 top, State Farm/Creative Commons; 12 top left, Jon Naustdalslid/Shutterstock; 12 top middle, 12 middle center, William A. Morgan/Shutterstock.com; 12 top right, Bilanol/Shutterstock; 12 middle right, Dustie/Shutterstock; 13 top right, Luis Viegas/Shutterstock; 13 bottom, Ulrike Stein/Shutterstock.com; 13 bottom left, Pongchart B/Shutterstock; 14 top, Dan Craggs/Creative Commons; 14 bottom, Palbert01/Creative Commons;14 bottom left, BearFotos/Shutterstock; 14 bottom right, Oqbas/Shutterstock; 16,17, swa182/Shutterstock; 16 bottom, stockyimages/Shutterstock; 17 top, Konmac/Shutterstock; 17 top left, ZaitsevMaksym/Shutterstock; 17 top right, LifetimeStock/Shutterstock; 17 middle, muratart/Shutterstock; 17 bottom left, Prostock-studio/Shutterstock; 17 bottom right, NASA/Public Domain;18 top, Skatebiker/Public Domain; 18 bottom, Punta Gorda Police Department/Public Domain; 18 bottom left, WilleeCole Photography/Shutterstock; 18 bottom right, Greg Patton/Shutterstock; 19 top, NOAA/OMAO/Melody Ovard/Creative Commons; 19 middle, Photick/Shutterstock; 19 bottom, Dan Borsum, NOAA/NWS/WR/WFO/Billings Montana/Creative Commons; 20, GerritR/Creative Commons; 20 bottom left, Krakenimages.com/Shutterstock; 20 bottom right, Roman Chazov/Shutterstock; 21 top, Anthony Quintano/Creative Commons; 21 bottom, 23 top, VORTEX II/Creative Commons; 21 bottom middle, Odua Images/Shutterstock; 22 OAA National Severe Storms Laboratory/Public Domain; 23 top left, Kamenetskiy Konstantin/Shutterstock; 23 top right, fizkes/Shutterstock; 23 bottom, James Bastow/Creative Commons; 24 top, 24 bottom, Courtesy: Jackson County Historical Society, Murphysboro, Illinois; 25 top, Benjamin Simeneta/Shutterstock; 25 top left, kimberrywood/Shutterstock; 25 top right, spaxiax/Shutterstock; 25 middle, Bob Webster/Creative Commons; 25 Nick Nolte/Creative Commons; 25 bottom left, i_am_zews/Shutterstock; 25 bottom right, Maridav/Shutterstock; 26 Krista Abel/Shutterstock; 26 bottom left, Evgenyrychko/Shutterstock; 26 bottom right, Dragon Images/Shutterstock; 27 top, Artazum/Shutterstock; 27 top right, Monkey Business Images/Shutterstock; 27 middle, Cheryl A. Meyer/Shutterstock; 27 bottom, ungvar/Shutterstock; 28 top left, Justin Hobson/Shutterstock; 28 bottom left, 28 bottom middle, stuar/Shutterstock; LEONARDO VITI/Shutterstock; 28-29, Austen Photography

Bearport Publishing Company Product Development Team
President: Jen Jenson; Director of Product Development: Spencer Brinker; Managing Editor: Allison Juda; Associate Editor: Naomi Reich; Associate Editor: Tiana Tran; Senior Designer: Colin O'Dea; Associate Designer: Elena Klinkner; Associate Designer: Kayla Eggert; Product Development Specialist: Anita Stasson

Produced for Bearport Publishing by BlueAppleWorks Inc.
Managing Editor for BlueAppleWorks: Melissa McClellan
Art Director: T.J. Choleva
Photo Research: Jane Reid

Library of Congress Cataloging-in-Publication Data

Names: Abramson, Marcia, 1949- author.
Title: Tornadoes / by Marcia Abramson.
Description: Minneapolis, Minnesota : Bearport Publishing Company, [2024] | Series: X-treme facts: natural disasters | Includes bibliographical references and index.
Identifiers: LCCN 2023005389 (print) | LCCN 2023005390 (ebook) | ISBN 9798885099806 (library binding) | ISBN 9798888221600 (paperback) | ISBN 9798888223000 (ebook)
Subjects: LCSH: Tornadoes--Juvenile literature.
Classification: LCC QC955.2 .A27 2024 (print) | LCC QC955.2 (ebook) | DDC 551.55/3--dc23/eng/20230207
LC record available at https://lccn.loc.gov/2023005389
LC ebook record available at https://lccn.loc.gov/2023005390

Copyright © 2024 Bearport Publishing Company. All rights reserved. No part of this publication may be reproduced in whole or in part, stored in any retrieval system, or transmitted in any form or by any means, electronic, mechanical, photocopying, recording, or otherwise, without written permission from the publisher.

For more information, write to Bearport Publishing, 5357 Penn Avenue South, Minneapolis, MN 55419.

Contents

Tornado Terror 4
Shape Shifters 6
The Birth of a Tornado 8
Fast and Furious 10
Meet Mr. Tornado 12
Tornado Alley 14
Too Many Tornadoes! 16
Freaky Funnels 18
Eyes on the Skies 20
Chasing Danger 22
Wicked Twisters 24
Seek Shelter! 26

Tornado in a Bottle 28
Glossary 30
Read More 31
Learn More Online 31
Index 32
About the Author 32

Tornado Terror

Dark, heavy clouds are rolling in. The air feels warm, thick, and damp. Birds and small animals disappear into their hiding places. A sound like a freight train is getting closer and closer as a swirling tower of dust and **debris** travels across the ground. It's a tornado. Take cover!

One of the earliest tornadoes ever recorded struck Germany in 788 CE.

The United States gets more tornadoes than anywhere else in the world—about 1,200 every year.

Powerful tornadoes can pick up cows, people, and even cars. The farthest an object has been carried is more than 200 miles (320 km)!

The wind speed inside a tornado can reach 300 miles per hour (480 kph). That's as fast as the world's fastest sports car.

Shape Shifters

Tornadoes are known for their towering, twisting shapes, but these storms aren't all the same. As a twisting storm drops from a cloud in the sky and makes contact with the ground, it can be wide or skinny, tall or short. No matter the shape of the storm, the bottom of a funnel cloud can cause serious damage as it rips and roars across the landscape.

The name tornado comes from the Spanish *tronar*, which means to thunder or roar.

Because of the way the storm cloud spins into a funnel shape, **tornadoes are sometimes called twisters.**

Often, a twister starts as a thin rope tornado and stays that way.

A **stovepipe tornado** is shaped like a **cylinder**. It has the same width from top to bottom.

WHAT A GRAND STOVEPIPE TORNADO!

YOUR HAT'S NOT TOO SHABBY EITHER, SIR!

Tornadoes can look gray, black, brown, blue, red, or green depending on the color of the dust and debris they have sucked up.

When two or more twisters drop down from the same parent cloud, it's called a multiple-**vortex** tornado.

Two tornadoes **spawned** from different parent clouds but spinning near each other are named **satellite tornadoes**.

Wedge tornadoes look at least as wide as they are tall. They can be a half mile (800 m) wide or more at their base.

THAT WEDGE TORNADO IS AFTER US!

DO YOU THINK IT COULD GIVE US A WEDGIE?

The Birth of a Tornado

All tornadoes are born in the same way. They form inside ordinary thunderclouds when warm, moist air rises and collides with cooler, drier air that is falling. This collision makes the thundercloud begin to spin. When the rotation combines with high winds, water in the air turns into cloud droplets that are spun into a funnel cloud. The funnel drops from the storm cloud all the way down to the ground.

To be considered a tornado, a funnel cloud must be in contact both with the ground below and storm cloud above.

Tornadoes usually spin counterclockwise in the Northern Hemisphere and clockwise in the Southern Hemisphere.

Most tornadoes are spawned by **supercells**—large, rotating thunderstorms formed by winds blowing in opposite directions.

An average tornado travels about 20 miles per hour (30 kph), but some tornadoes can go more than 60 miles per hour (95 kph).

Non-supercell tornadoes—about one out of every five twisters—**come from a line of fast-moving thunderstorms.**

THAT TORNADO IS SPEEDING!

WELL, CAN YOU ARREST IT?

Fast and Furious

A tornado forming is dramatic, dropping down to Earth with a roar. After doing its damage, however, it leaves with a whimper. The winds that drive the tornado's rotation weaken, the twister shrinks and disappears altogether. But even a short-lived tornado can do a lot of damage very quickly.

Tornadoes can tear across land for just a few minutes or can last for a few hours!

Extreme tornadoes may travel 100 miles (160 km) or more before they break up.

Most tornadoes stay on the ground for 5 to 10 minutes.

Twisters don't always move in a straight line! They can turn sharply and reverse course.

Because of its unpredictable path, a tornado may destroy one house while the one next door is fine.

In December 2021, a tornado raged for four hours, destroying **the town of Mayfield, Kentucky.**

An average tornado in the United States is about **400 yards (350 meters) wide** and travels on the ground for 5 miles (8 km).

Meet Mr. Tornado

People have always known that tornadoes are fast and furious. But there used to be no **accurate** way to measure the wind speeds that made them so destructive. It wasn't until 1971 that **meteorologist** Tetsuya Theodore Fujita developed a scale to measure tornado intensity. He studied damage to buildings and crops, information from weather **radar**, eyewitness and news reports, and the ground swirl patterns left behind by tornadoes. Using all this information, Fujita was able to estimate the tornado's wind speed.

In 2007, the American Meteorological Society began using the Enhanced Fujita scale, a more accurate ranking of the levels of damage caused by tornadoes.

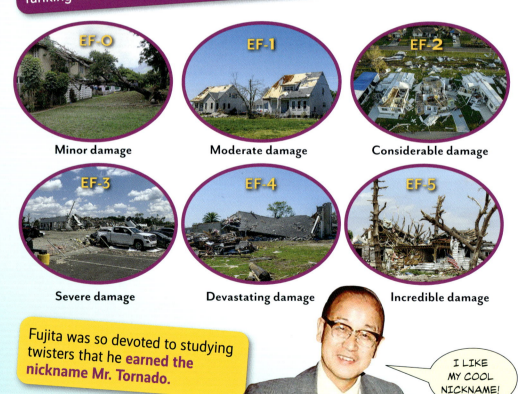

EF-0 Minor damage
EF-1 Moderate damage
EF-2 Considerable damage
EF-3 Severe damage
EF-4 Devastating damage
EF-5 Incredible damage

Fujita was so devoted to studying twisters that he **earned the nickname Mr. Tornado.**

I LIKE MY COOL NICKNAME!

Fujita was among the first to fly over storm-hit areas to study tornado damage and map tornado paths.

YUP, THIS PLACE WAS HIT BY A MULTI-FUNNEL TORNADO!

Fujita helped discover that most damaging tornadoes were actually made up of several small funnels rotating within a parent cloud.

Air travelers can thank Fujita for discovering downbursts. These very powerful winds can drop down from a thunderstorm and make airplanes crash to the ground.

Today, pilot training and airport safety **procedures** are based upon Fujita's research.

SHOULD I BE WORRIED ABOUT BAD WEATHER?

NOT AT ALL! THANKS TO MR. TORNADO, OUR PILOTS CAN HANDLE ANY STORM!

Tornado Alley

Mr. Tornado lived and worked in Chicago, Illinois. The Windy City, as Chicago has been nicknamed, isn't far from Tornado Alley. This stretch of land in the center of the United States gets about 350 twisters a year. Tornadoes form in this area when cool air from the Rocky Mountains runs into warm, moist air from the Gulf of Mexico.

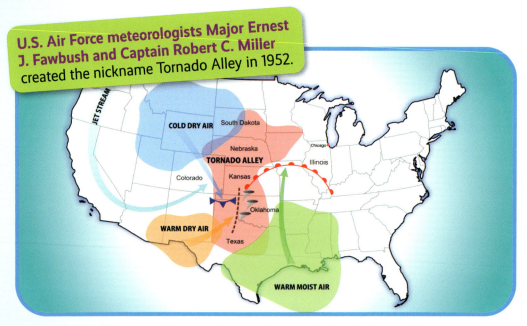

U.S. Air Force meteorologists Major Ernest J. Fawbush and Captain Robert C. Miller created the nickname Tornado Alley in 1952.

Texas gets the most tornadoes of any state, followed by Kansas.

THE TWIST IS MY BIRTHDAY DANCE!

LET ME GUESS... YOU WERE BORN ON MAY 20TH!

The Tornado Alley town of Codell, Kansas, was struck by twisters on May 20 in 1916, 1917, and 1918!

14

Rhode Island has the fewest reported tornadoes in the United States.

Too Many Tornadoes!

Many twisters may form at the same time in parts of Tornado Alley. This is called a super outbreak. Over two days in December 2021, 61 tornadoes killed 80 people in 8 states. The total number of tornadoes per year has not changed much, but there are now fewer days with just one tornado reported than there are days with thirty or more spotted!

A three-day super outbreak in April 2011 sent a record 360 tornadoes tearing across the United States and Canada.

On April 3, 1974, 21 tornadoes roared across Indiana at the same time

HEY, STORM! WHY DO YOU SPAWN SO MANY TORNADOES?!

BECAUSE IT'S RIGHT UP MY ALLEY!

England—not anywhere in Tornado Alley—holds the record for most tornadoes in the shortest period of time, with 104 forming in less than 6 hours.

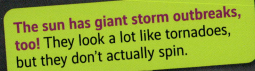

The sun has giant storm outbreaks, too! They look a lot like tornadoes, but they don't actually spin.

Hurricanes can spawn many tornadoes. Hurricane Ivan set the record with 120 in September 2004.

17

Freaky Funnels

Super outbreaks are not something you ever want to witness. But imagine seeing a twister over the ocean. This is called a waterspout. Can you picture a funnel cloud made of fire or snow? That can happen, too! Some spinning storms pick up more than just dust and debris. Check out these terrible twisters.

Many waterspouts are weaker than land tornadoes, but they can still harm swimmers, ships, and aircraft.

Waterspouts that form from severe thunderstorms are more powerful, longer lasting, and more destructive.

Although unsuccessful, folks in the **Florida Keys** once tried to break up a waterspout by firing a cannonball into it.

THAT WATERSPOUT IS MOVING TOWARD US. SHOULD WE FIRE AT IT?

DON'T BOTHER! THAT DOESN'T WORK.

Winds in an extreme waterspout can blow up to 150 miles per hour (240 kph).

Snownadoes form when fog rising over snow is sent spinning by cold, strong winds. The rotating mist picks up loose snow and forms a tornado-like funnel shape.

During a wildfire, extreme heat rises and can be spun around by strong winds, drawing flame and ash into its vortex. The result is a firenado.

Snownadoes, firenadoes, and many waterspouts are not true tornadoes since they do not form and drop down from rotating thunderstorms.

Eyes on the Skies

Whether a short-lived waterspout or a super outbreak of tornadoes, these twisty storms can cause serious damage and threaten lives. Luckily, today's weather forecasters have tools for detecting tornadoes and sending out early warnings. **Doppler radar** helps track the speed, direction, and rotation of winds that might produce tornadoes. But some tornadoes form very quickly, so nothing beats a weather watcher with eyes on the sky!

The SKYWARN network relies on nearly 400,000 ordinary people who watch for tornadoes.

WHAT ARE YOU WAITING FOR? JOIN THE TEAM!

The National Weather Service (NWS) encourages people who work in schools, hospitals, nursing homes, and other public buildings to become storm spotters.

When storm spotters see severe weather, **they notify their local weather service offices.**

I'D BETTER CALL THE WEATHER SERVICE ABOUT THIS STORM!

Once notified by storm spotters, the local weather service activates emergency alerts and sends a report to the NWS.

Tornado warnings get to the public through television, radio, computer, and text alerts.

SKYWARN storm spotters learn how to stay safe. They must be trained and take a two-hour class.

WHO IS TEXTING YOU?

IT'S THE WEATHER SERVICE. THERE'S A TORNADO!

Chasing Danger

Most storm spotters keep an eye on the sky from within the safety of their homes or workplaces. But more serious storm chasers hop in their cars to drive toward the action. Storm chasers use **GPS**, weather reports, and Doppler radar to track twisters and other strong storms. They travel in strong, heavy vehicles and try to get up close and personal with the monster storms.

Most storm chasers are trained professionals who are paid to collect storm **data** that will help researchers learn more about severe weather.

Weather researchers launch mini-weather balloons into rotating thunderstorms to learn more about how tornadoes form.

Storm chasing is extremely dangerous. Only weather experts with safety training should try it.

American storm chaser Roger Hill has tracked down more than 750 tornadoes, setting a world record.

Scientists now use remote-controlled drones to study tornadoes that are difficult to reach.

Wicked Twisters

When a tornado roars through a town, roads are torn up, businesses are destroyed, houses are flattened, and possessions are scattered. Worst of all, lives are lost. With today's more accurate forecasts, earlier warnings, and stronger buildings, tornadoes are now killing fewer people. Still, these storms pack a punch.

The Tri-State Tornado of 1925 raged across Missouri, Illinois, and Indiana. It was the deadliest twister in the U.S., killing 695 people and injuring 2,207.

The Tri-State Tornado's path of destruction was more than 200 miles (320 km) long, making researchers think it was actually made up of multiple tornadoes.

The world's deadliest tornado hit Bangladesh on April 26, 1989, killing 1,300 people.

Tornadoes have picked up whole houses and set them down somewhere else entirely.

A tornado sucked Matt Suter of Missouri from his trailer and carried him 1,307 feet (398 m) in 2006. He was okay—and set a record!

One of the most devastating multiple-vortex tornadoes of all time destroyed a quarter of Joplin, Missouri, on May 22, 2011.

The El Reno Tornado was the widest twister ever recorded at 2.6 miles (4.2 km) across!

Seek Shelter!

Tornadoes can develop and strike very quickly. So, if your family lives in an area where twisters are possible, you need an emergency plan. Once a tornado warning has been issued, you should immediately seek shelter. Go to a room on the lowest floor of the building that has no windows and does not share a wall with the outside of the house. Being prepared can go a long way to keep you safe!

Wrapping yourself in blankets and coats can help protect you from flying glass, wood, and other debris.

Tornado in a Bottle

Activity

You can create the perfect conditions for a tornado right in your kitchen! See the spiral of the storm for yourself using just a few supplies!

A tornado may look almost see-through until debris is picked up by the funnel.

What You Will Need

- 2 clear plastic 2-liter bottles that are empty
- Water
- Food coloring in your favorite color
- Dish detergent
- A tornado tube connector or duct tape

Rotating thunderstorms that include severe winds, lightning, and hail usually lead to a tornado build up.

Step One

Fill one bottle with water about three-quarters full. Add a couple of drops of food coloring and one drop of dish detergent.

Step Two

If you are using a connector, screw the tornado tube connector onto the bottle. Otherwise, skip this step.

Step Three

If you're using a connector, screw the second bottle on top of the tornado tube. Make sure it's tight so nothing leaks. If you're using duct tape, place the second bottle on top of the one with water. Wrap the tape around both bottle tops to secure them tightly.

Step Four

Turn the bottles over so that the empty one is at the bottom. Move the bottle rapidly in a circle to start a vortex. After a few seconds, you will see the water begin swirling. Stop, and watch your tornado twist away!

accurate free from mistakes

armored protected by a strong outer covering

cylinder a column-like shape

data information and facts, such as measurements

debris scattered pieces of something that has been destroyed or damaged

Doppler radar a system that finds objects and measures their speed

Florida Keys the long series of small, narrow islands at the southern tip of Florida

GPS Global Positioning System; a space-based navigation satellite system that provides accurate location information

meteorologist someone who studies the atmosphere, weather, and weather forecasting

procedures steps or sets of instructions to follow in order

radar a system that uses radio waves to find moving objects in the sky

satellite tornadoes smaller twisters that revolve near and around larger ones

spawned produced or gave birth to, especially in large numbers

supercells weather systems with strong, rotating winds and thunderstorms

vortex a whirling, twisting, spinning mass

Read More

Bergin, Raymond. *Terrible Storms (What on Earth? Climate Change Explained).* Minneapolis: Bearport Publishing, 2022.

Challoner, Jack. *Hurricane & Tornado (DK Eyewitness).* New York: DK Publishing, 2021.

Crane, Cody. *All about Tornadoes (A True Book: Natural Disaster!).* New York: Children's Press, 2021.

Learn More Online

1. Go to **www.factsurfer.com** or scan the QR code below.

2. Enter **"X-treme Tornadoes"** into the search box.

3. Click on the cover of this book to see a list of websites.

Index

chasers 22–24
clouds 4–9, 13, 15, 18
damage 6, 10, 12–13, 20, 24–25
debris 4, 7, 18, 27–28
destruction 12, 18, 24
emergency 21, 26–27
firenadoes 19
forecast 14, 20, 24
funnel cloud 6, 8, 15, 18
houses 11, 24–27
Mr. Tornado 12–14
outbreak 16–18, 20
path 11, 13, 24
radar 12, 20, 22

rotation 8–10, 13, 19–20, 22, 28
shelter 23, 26–27
snownadoes 19
spotters 20–22, 24
supercell 9
thunderstorm 9, 13, 18–19, 22, 28
Tornado Alley 14, 16–17
training 13, 21–22
vortex 7, 19, 25, 29
warning 20–21, 24, 26
waterspout 18–20
weather service 20–21
wind 5, 8–10, 12–14, 19–20, 23, 27–28

About the Author

Marcia Abramson lives in Ann Arbor, Michigan. It's not in Tornado Alley but still gets twisters. She has seen one from a distance. She's also waited out lots of warnings in the basement!